HOW TO SURVIVE A
LAWYER

Smile —
They don't.
Write books like
this for every
profession —

You're just
special

Love —
ME

I had a
LAWYER
once.

HOW TO SURVIVE A
LAWYER

STEPHEN BAKER

Illustrated by Rick Penn-Kraus

PRICE STERN SLOAN
Los Angeles

Text © 1991 by Stephen Baker
Illustrations © 1991 by Price Stern Sloan, Inc.
Published by Price Stern Sloan, Inc.
11150 Olympic Boulevard, Suite 650
Los Angeles, California 90064
Printed in the U.S.A.

10 9 8 7 6 5 4 3 2 1

All rights reserved. No part of this publication may be reproduced, stored in a retrieval system or transmitted, in any form or by any means, electronic, mechanical, photocopying, recording or otherwise, without the prior written permission of the publisher.

Library of Congress Cataloging in Publication
Baker, Stephen, 1921-
How to survive a lawyer/by Stephen Baker
p. cm.
ISBN 0-8431-2896-8
1. Lawyers—Humor. 2. Lawyers—Psychology—Humor. 3. American wit and humor. I. Title.
PN6231.L4B34 1991
818'.5402—dc20   91-14673
CIP

Note: The masculine pronoun "he" is used in this book for grammatical convenience only. No sexism is intended. Anything said about members of the legal profession applies equally to both men and women in pursuit of justice and billable hours.

This book has been printed on acid-free paper.

The first thing we do is kill all lawyers.
William Shakespeare

The second thing we do is put them six feet under.
Stephen Baker

Table of Contents

PREFACE

EVERYBODY needs a lawyer sooner or later. He is the person always there when you need him. Or even when you don't.

Think about it. Sure, you can run to your preacher or rabbi for advice in your quest for justice only to be told, "Hey, turn the other cheek." Exactly the words you least want to hear. Or you can visit your therapist who will take copious notes of your grievances at his going rate and say absolutely nothing during the entire session. Forget about your friends; their problems are more serious than yours. Your barkeep responds with his usual "How you doin'?" and walks away before you have a chance to answer his question. Your spouse hasn't talked to you in months, and your beaming taxi driver speaks nary a word of English.

Clearly, that leaves the lawyer as your only choice. So you find out who is the best in town, and call him for an appointment. There goes the first myth about the profession —that lawyers are too busy to talk to clients on the telephone. Not this one. He lets you know you caught him just as he was about to leave for court but, considering your situation, he will rearrange his schedule. Always, he is prepared to share this time with anyone in need of help, especially if that person could turn out to be a future client.

Your breathing improves noticeably as you talk to your counsel-to-be. You decide not to go to Brazil after all, or even stop at your favorite pub on your way to his office. Your lawyer is a human being, one of the thousand lights. He cares about people, in this instance, you. And as you meet him one-on-one, sitting across his desk, you discover that there is even more to him than that. He is a quick study, probably a genius. Without so much as asking you a single question, he already knows all about the ramifications of your case.

"There's nothing new under the sun," he tells you. "Our office handled thousands of cases exactly like yours," he explains.

"Exactly?" you ask.

"Exactly."

Obviously, you are talking to the right person. You're in luck. You can't help but be impressed by his equanimity in the face of adversity. The world that lay in ruins just moments ago is coming together again.

Not to suggest he is a know-it-all. He is accustomed to plumbing the deepest depths. True to his calling, he looks at problems from every angle, always in the hopes of discovering previously hidden evidence. His questions are sharp and to the point.

"Would you like some coffee?" he asks.

You nod in the affirmative. At this point you welcome any beverage, even non-alcoholic.

He touches one of the many call buttons on his intercom and his secretary materializes at the door with a beautific smile glued to her face. Your lawyer perseveres. "How do you like it? Cream? Milk? Black?"

While you're searching for the right answer, he shoots another one at you. "Sugar?" No detail is too small for this counsel.

Over a cup of coffee, he asks you a few more questions equally tantalizing, probably to find out what kind of person he is about to do business with. Legal problems, after all, can be emotionally draining; he doesn't want a client collapsing into his arms halfway through the case. For the most part, the information has to do with your innermost character; your earning capacity, cash value of your investments, size of your bank account and the ability of your estate to cover his expenses in case of your untimely demise. He then tells you all *you* need to know about winning your case: His complete background, beginning with his years in kindergarten; the origins of the framed certificates hanging on the wall; names of politicians, judges, mayors, city comptrollers, and the Inspector General of the Sanitation Bureau, whose pictures adorn his office with him standing by their sides; dates of articles in *The National Law Journal, Lawyers Weekly, American Lawyer, Law Review, Columbia Law Journal* on cases he won; the appalling lack of competence of everyone else in his profession; his pay-in-advance billing procedure; his participation in an upcoming pro-am tennis tournament; and the marked improvement in his game brought about by changing his thumb position on the racket.

This is no small amount of information for a layman to absorb in so short a time. But you try anyway. A few days after your meeting, you find a letter in your mailbox from his office. You open the envelope with some trepidation. No doubt what you're holding in your hands is a progress report, the first of many more to come. Inside you find a bill for two-and-a-half hours of legal consultation.

Who says lawyers don't keep track of things?

Chapter 1

In God We Trust

THIS motto hangs high on the walls of courtrooms everywhere; lawyers welcome it with a smile. These words warm their hearts, not to mention their pocketbooks. These words confirm what they have been telling their clients all along: Have faith in the One Above, who happens to be none other than present counsel.

A lawyer's identification with God is to be expected. The rest of us have role models, such as Albert Schweitzer, Mother Teresa or the President of the United States. No such earthly creatures quite live up to lawyers' standards, however. They go for the best. God will do.

True, striking similarities exist between God and lawyers. They act, and sometimes even look, alike. They talk in the same tone of voice. They insist on obedience. And, they are both all-knowing (although most lawyers will concede that they know a little more). However, the latter's advice is billable, of course.

Even more remarkable is their shared proclivity to put everything in writing, especially when it concerns matters of importance, such as who is going to pay for local telephone calls. About the only difference

1

is in the medium they use. God prefers stone tablets for delivering messages. Lawyers go for paper, which is easier to put in a briefcase, in a fax machine or in a No. 10 billing envelope.

To hear lawyers tell it, in some ways they're actually one up on their counterpart in the world above. Take the Ten Commandments. While lawyers admit that this document has merit, they still have a problem with its language. It simply lacks specifics; it would not hold up in court. Plainly, God had poor legal counsel in drafting the covenant — which is not too surprising, given the fact that there are no lawyers in Heaven.

Another similarity is that both God and lawyers are omnipresent. His is an ubiquitous presence; lawyers—less so. But they manage to appear at a moment's notice just the same, say at the scene of an airplane accident, the funeral services of a rich uncle or a corporate proxy battle.

With so much in common, it is easy to see why God and lawyers should so easily be confused with one another. Appearances notwithstanding, differences do exist, however. The list on the next page may be helpful for quick reference.

HOW TO TELL THEM APART

GOD

Sits on a throne.

Lives in the clouds.

Rests on the Seventh Day.

Welcomes sacramental offerings.

Has angels take care of the details.

Makes sure His followers do not have to wait long at the Pearly Gates.

Blesses the poor.

Answers calls.

LAWYERS

Sit in a swivel chair.

Have only their heads in the clouds.

Rest for six days a week, to summon up energy for a golf game on the Seventh Day.

Welcome cash, checks and all major credit cards.

Have associates take care of the details.

Make sure their clients have long waits in the reception room.

Refer the poor to the Legal Aid.

Do not answer calls.

SUMMARY

1. God moves in mysterious ways. So do lawyers.

2. God created Man in His own image. Lawyers created God in theirs.

3. Never make the sign of the cross before your lawyer. Try a dollar sign instead.

4. Most lawyers resent comparisons between themselves and God. Plainly, they feel superior to Him.

5. It simply isn't true that lawyers like to play God. They *are* God—as their clients find out all too soon.

Chapter 2

How Lawyers Get That Way

FOR a lawyer to pursue his calling successfully, it is important that he should feel *genuinely* hostile toward all his fellow beings. Note the emphasis on the word "genuinely." For the feeling must be absolute and all-pervasive; it must be a passion with him. His venom must be directed against all creatures, including judges, jurists and most of all, you, the client. Good lawyers also detest members of their own family, pets and living plants. Their favorite fantasy is to drag each and every living thing they see through the court system, with them acting as prosecutors.

Real lawyers start hating people the very moment they open their eyes in the morning and look around. Thoughts of destruction enter their minds almost immediately. This gives them the impetus to leap out of bed, run around the room and scream at no one in particular. They shave quickly, then take a shower, throw on some clothes and hurry out the door to give vent to their animosity for the rest of the day.

It so happens, lawyers have every reason to be frustrated. Their occupation is a heavy burden for them to carry all day, particularly if one considers that some lawyers work for less than $250 an hour. Just imagine having to go through a day like this:

THE LAWYER'S SCHEDULE

9:30 A.M.	Lawyer arrives in his office.
9:35 A.M.	He asks for his morning coffee. Secretary brings it to him.
9:38 A.M.	He complains about lack of sugar in his coffee.
9:45-9:50 A.M.	Secretary prepares another cup, puts more sugar in it.
9:50-10:15 A.M.	Lawyer notes with satisfaction, sipping the beverage. He reads *The Wall Street Journal.*
10:30-11:30 A.M.	Lawyer appears in court to submit a motion. He arrives at second roll calling, sits down and continues to read the paper.
11:31 A.M.	Bailiff calls "No reading of newspapers, please. Order in the Court."
11:35 A.M.-12:00 P.M.	Lawyer leaves courtroom and finishes reading in the hallway.
12:05-12:15 P.M.	Lawyer calls his stockbroker on public phone making notes.
12:16-12:30 P.M.	He returns to courtroom, waiting to be called.
12:31-12:35 P.M.	Lawyer is called to the bench to submit a Request for Postponement. Opposing lawyer puts forth an Answer. Judge asks, "Four weeks will be all right with both sides?"
12:36-1:00 P.M.	Two lawyers grin at one another, walk down the aisle engrossed in conversation.

1:01 P.M.	They have lunch at their favorite restaurant a few blocks away.
1:15 P.M.	They agree to share a bottle of Heitz Cabernet Sauvignon Special Selection '85.
1:16-1:30 P.M.	Discussion centers on comparing performance between Acura Legend Coupe, Mercedes 300E and BMW 535.
1:31-1:45 P.M.	They agree on a 10:30 A.M. tee-off time this coming Thursday at lawyer's country club.
2:00 P.M.	Lawyer returns to his office.
2:35-3:50 P.M.	Secretary asks if he wishes to respond to any of the phone messages received while he was away. Lawyer goes through the list of calls carefully.
3:55-4:40 P.M.	He returns one call, to a lady friend. He closes his office door while he is on the phone. The two set up a dinner date for the evening.
4:45-5:00 P.M.	Secretary has lawyer look over his time sheet. Lawyer adds day's billable hours so far. Five hours multiplied by two: time spent in court, and time spent thinking about the problems of another client during the same morning hours.
5:01-5:05 P.M.	Associate enters with a proposal, concerning the filing of a class action suit on behalf of the Animal Rights Foundation regarding the killing of cockroaches in high-rise apartment buildings. Members of the Foundation have already agreed to contribute toward legal expenses. Lawyer smiles and says, "Good work. You're thinking."

5:10-5:30 P.M.	Lawyer calls a potential client to see if she has already filed for divorce. He says he knows just the attorney to handle the case. Potential client announces she and her husband are considering reconciliation. Lawyer tells her she is making a big mistake. She says she wants to give it a try. She still loves her husband. Lawyer says, "Love is blind, isn't it?" Her voice trembles as she says she will think about his comments and promises to call him back soon.
5:36 P.M.	Lawyer puts down two more billable hours on his time sheet.
5:40 P.M.	Lawyer asks his secretary to call his wife and tell her that he will be late tonight on account of his schedule.
6:30 P.M.	Lawyer meets woman friend at a corner table in a restaurant.
8:30 P.M.	Woman friend moves her chair closer as she sips her drink, the sixth one for the evening.
9:15 P.M.	The two leave the restaurant laughing.

With that kind of a schedule, day after day after day, it is little wonder that so many lawyers are on the verge of an emotional breakdown. No human being could long endure such pressure.

There are those who believe lawyers are not born hostile; these observers argue that it is the years in their chosen profession that turns them ornery. They may have a point there. It seems the process starts early in life, at two or three minutes after birth. Yanked into daylight by pairs of rubber-sheathed hands, cleansed and dried without as much as being consulted, it soon becomes clear to the newborn that his best defense in life will be to take the offense. It is at this point that lawyers usually decide on their future career.

The lawyer is at odds with the world even while still lying in the crib. He reaches out to grab at anything within arm's range, especially

if the item is of value, such as visitors' pocketbooks, wallets or jewelry. His screams are louder than any other baby's in the maternity ward and are delivered at a higher pitch. His vocal skills serve him well; they help him to develop a sense of power, a sphere of influence. Nurses respond to his shrieks as they come running to find out what seems to be the trouble. They shower him with kindness. Most of them opt for earmuffs to prevent permanent hearing loss.

In the years that follow, he continues to hone his magisterial talents at every opportunity. In his fights with his contemporaries, he relies more on his mouth than his fists. He complains a lot and prefers taking the role of the aggrieved party. His favorite Christmas toy is a battery-operated toy ambulance, which he likes to chase all over the living room.

In his teens, he begins to act much like a true lawyer. Many parents feel at this point that they have a problem child on their hands. They may even turn to therapy for their offspring only to be told not to worry. To put it simply: they are but privy to the normal growing up process of an aspiring lawyer, who is beginning to use what nature giveth.

SIGNS OF PROMISING LEGAL TALENT

More than five affirmative answers bodes a bright future for lawyers-to-be.

	Yes	No
At birth:		
• Enters this world screaming louder than other newborns.	❏	❏
• Spits at the nurse holding him.	❏	❏
• Frowns at his mother.	❏	❏
Age 1 to 4:		
• Enjoys playing with dollar bills.	❏	❏
• Breaks piggy bank to find out what it holds.	❏	❏
• Wants to mix his milk with hard liquor.	❏	❏
Age 4 to 8:		
• Favorite color is green.	❏	❏
• Kicks his dog.	❏	❏
• Charges twenty-five cents a minute for giving advice.	❏	❏
• Arranges a merger among lemonade stands in the neighborhood electing himself chief executive officer.	❏	❏
Age 8 to 14:		
• Breaks record for writing the longest sentence in his English 101 class.	❏	❏
• Refers to his room as his "domicile."	❏	❏
• Keeps a cluttered desktop.	❏	❏
Age 14 to 18:		
• Cites his First Amendment Rights when asked to take out the garbage.	❏	❏
• Insists on keeping a copy of his parents' last will in his file.	❏	❏
• Enlists the services of a certified public accountant to help him list his "deductibles" on his personal income tax return.	❏	❏

SUMMARY

1. Lawyers start screaming as babies and keep on doing so for the rest of their lives.

2. A lawyer's favorite game as a child is hide-and-seek. It is his first training experience as a professional.

3. As lawyers grow up, changing from baby talk to legalese presents no problem.

4. The only lawyer better than a born lawyer is one not yet born.

Chapter 3

How to Recognize a Lawyer

L AWYERS are readily identifiable from both near and far distances by the way they comport themselves. Their manner of moving backwards and—most of the time—sideways as they walk is typical of the species. Their gait is brisk with the body slightly leaning forward as if fighting the wind. Their carriage suggests a sense of purpose, impressing clients who like to see their lawyer able to follow directions.

Actually, most lawyers have a good reason to be in a hurry. They are eager to find a place where they can sit down and take the load off their feet; walking from here to there consumes energy. Sitting is a more natural—and from the lawyer's point of view, much more desirable—posture. The position allows them to make phone calls (all lawyers' outgoing phone calls need immediate attention), to take notes on a legal pad, and most of all, to stare in the face of their clients or whomever it is they're talking to.

All lawyers stare. The average person looks or peers but this is not so of members of the legal profession. Their intensity is understandable. While those in less demanding occupations use their eyes chiefly for the purpose of receiving visual information, lawyers use their penetrating looks to let others know how they feel about them.

THE LAWYER'S LOOKS

THE ONCE-OVER is to see if you're for real. Rumor has it that experienced lawyers can size up their clients' ability to pay at a single glance.

THE SUSPICIOUS GLINT usually follows the ONCE-OVER. Lawyers wonder if the client will pay his bills on time.

THE LEER reminds a client that when it comes to law, the lawyer has the last word.

THE LOOK OF DISDAIN is a lawyer's reflex to his client's suggestion that perhaps the case should be settled out of court.

Lawyers can also be recognized by their facial expressions. These they develop through the years by practicing in front of the mirror every morning. The idea is always the same: to put the client in his place. By far the most popular is the PAINED LOOK—a world-weary expression that suggests having seen it all. The more seasoned the lawyer, the more distressed his appearance will be, no doubt reflecting the burdens that fall upon him.

ONE YEAR   **FIVE YEARS**   **TWENTY YEARS**

Women lawyers manage to keep their smiles longer. Still, the smile turns into a grin, sooner or later, and finally, into a contentious sneer—the hallmark of the profession.

ONE YEAR   **FIVE YEARS**   **TWENTY YEARS**

While lawyers share much in common, it is still possible to tell them apart. With age, experience and increase of income, their body shapes change as may be expected.

LAW SCHOOL RECRUIT   **CLERK**

JUNIOR ASSOCIATE   **SENIOR ASSOCIATE**

Lawyers can also be distinguished from one another by their dress code. Their choices of apparel, as often as not, depend on the moment. Many maintain a large and varied wardrobe much like that of a versatile actor who may be called on stage to portray several characters in rapid succession.

THE CONSERVATIVE LOOK (MALE)

No hat

Peaked lapels

Button-down collar

Dark color, pinstripe

Designer label
inside jacket

Red or maroon
silk necktie

Matching
vest

Two pens in
vest pocket

Cufflinks,
preferably gold

Watch with
calendar window

Briefcase filled
with papers

Knee-length socks

Wingtip shoes
(just shined)

THE CONSERVATIVE LOOK
(FEMALE)

Tortoiseshell glasses

Pearl button earrings

Cultured pearl necklace

White silk blouse

Watch

Wedding ring

Grey/brown/navy jacket
(plain or pinstripe)

Grey/brown/navy
matching skirt

Briefcase matching suit color

Skirt length slightly below
the knee

Beige pantyhose

Patent leather pumps
with medium heels

THE CASUAL LOOK (MALE)

Sunglasses
(optional)

Long hair
(ribbon optional
in ducktail)

Beard or mustache

Lumber jacket
open at the neck
to display T-shirt
and hairy chest

Wide leather belt with
large buckle

Jeans, chinos or
corduroys

Crew socks

Duffel bag

Walking sneakers,
loafers or work shoes

THE CASUAL LOOK (FEMALE)

Scarf knotted at the neck

Cotton turtleneck

Chain with charm on it

Blazer

Designer watch

No wedding ring

Thrift shop skirt, preferably with flowered pattern

Large handbag

Low-heel shoes or sandals

Baggy pantyhose

SUSPENDERS: THE MOST TELLING FASHION STATEMENT OF ALL

A lawyer's suspenders are an important part of his wardrobe. Clarence Darrow was clever enough to wear them more than half a century ago at the John T. Scopes trial, thus reducing his chances of being caught with his pants down.

LAWYER'S DESK

First and foremost, a lawyer's office must exude an air of authority, particularly if its occupant does not. The height and length of the bookshelf reflects just that, as do the number of telephones on his desk, memorabilia on the walls and the shredder in the corner barely visible behind the rubber plants. This last item is an absolute necessity in conducting business everyday.

Papers stacked up high suggest the heavy workload of a sought-after lawyer. He may yet be willing to take on your case for just and adequate compensation.

LAWYER'S SWIVEL CHAIR

An important piece of furniture in a lawyer's office is his swivel chair. It is here that he spends a great deal of his time, making phone calls, holding conferences and filling out time sheets.

This piece of furniture has often been compared to the familiar rocking chair, but that no longer holds true. Today's swivel chair combines a variety of much-needed features, including those of a chaise lounge, a rowing exercise machine, a barber's chair, a bar stool and a Murphy bed.

A Pneumatic Height Adjustment Mechanism raises or lowers the seat at the touch of a forefinger. The lawyer can now stare down at his client from on high, or if he wishes, hide behind stacks of papers on the desk. Mobile Dual Wheel Castors make it possible for the occupant to travel across the room in a sitting position, even to accompany the client to the door.

SUMMARY

1. Most lawyers look intent. They're intent on making money.

2. Lawyers go by several names. First, last and middle, plus the names clients use when they receive their monthly statements.

3. Beware of the lawyer who smiles. Why is he smiling?

4. All lawyers' trousers are cut in the same manner. They have deep pockets.

5. First impressions are important. Try to look your best for the first interview with your lawyer.

Whereas the party of the first part and the
party of the second part will negotiate,
but not exclude, the third party's
Huh?

Chapter 4

Legalese Spoken Here

T would be highly unprofitable for lawyers to speak like most people do. Using shorter and fewer words to convey simple, straightforward thoughts would have serious consequences. Legal briefs would live up to their name; sheafs of legal documents would shrink to a few pages. The paper industry would suffer as a result. There would also be repercussions in the manufacturing of office staplers, copying machines and office liquor cabinets. The phone company would have to raise its rates to stay in business. Worst of all, clients might actually understand what their attorney was talking about—an ominous development.

A client's response such as, "I'm not sure if I understand," is exactly what the lawyer wants to hear. He will be quick to point out that his is an intricate profession and that you should not be concerned about your inability to decipher his statement. It is the way of the world.

Training in illegibility begins early on in the life of a lawyer. As an infant, he soon discovers that the sounds he produces—any kind of

29

sound—never fail to impress those who are important. So he keeps making them whenever he gets a chance. As he gets older, he finds that forming words and sentences can actually work against his own best interest; it is better to make no sense at all and keep others guessing. This revelation serves him well in his adult years, particularly with clients, meetings, business presentations or political rallies.

It is for this reason that law school puts so much emphasis on aspiring lawyers' ability to speak convincingly and at great length about absolutely nothing. These supplementary courses are especially popular among students:

5001 POLYSYLLABIC PRO-FUNDITIES are taught so that students are able to memorize words, or better still, make them up, of five to fifteen syllables–the longer, the better. Those able to come up with words over twenty syllables are invited to become editors on one of the law journals of the school and flaunt their skills.

PUNCTILIOUS PUNCTUATION is taught so that students learn to use commas in place of periods and are able to keep from ending a sentence. It is important that the student understand that "reduced to writing" does not mean that at all. To pass the final examination, the student must be able to write at least one sentence taking up the entire page.

BASIC BUNK sessions begin at normal room temperature and gradually heat up as students make their presentations. Classes are dismissed when the thermometer reaches 105°F.

ADVANCED DOUBLE TALK stresses total impenetrability. Top students in class may be chosen to deliver the next valedictory address to the entire student body, serving as an inspiration to all.

FOREIGN PHRASEOLOGY is designed to eliminate any remaining possibility of being understood. Exercises are given in plain legalese using phrases in Latin, French and—in New York City—Yiddish.

VOICE LESSONS aim to develop the ability to speak from the diaphragm, if not the brain. It is essential for a lawyer to be heard across the courtroom, across the street and from one end of the block to the other. The phrase "Objection, your Honor!" is practiced in a drawn-out whine.

HOW A LAWYER MAKES HIS POINT

With so few points to make, a lawyer's body language becomes ever so important in gaining attention.

OFFICE MARATHON calls for purposeful pacing back and forth in the office. Client follows lawyer's peripatetic exercise. Pivoting his head produces dizziness, extreme fatigue and complete disorientation—all of which will put him on the defensive.

HYPNOTIC TRANCES impale a client. Loss of memory works in lawyer's favor, enabling him to proceed without interruption.

VERTICAL TAKE-OFF wakes up client. Lawyer's feet leave the ground, while his flailing arms enable him to remain aloft for several seconds.

TEMPER TANTRUM helps lawyer to relieve nervous tension created by client's presence in office. Thick carpet protects him from injuring himself while thrashing on the floor.

There are times when your lawyer may actually stop talking, either to catch his breath or—more important for the client—to think. Moments of cogitation are rare, and they should be duly appreciated. It is difficult to tell, however, the difference between meditation and sleep. Much like certain animal species, lawyers have developed ways of sleeping with their eyes wide open. A better way to tell the difference is to listen and watch. Snoring suggests your lawyer has left the conscious world. Sliding off his chair is an even more definite sign that he has gone to sleep.

There is always the possibility that your lawyer has managed to retain consciousness; he may even be thinking about your problem. Shown here are signs of life.

HOW YOU CAN TELL YOUR LAWYER IS THINKING

Frown

Sweating brow

Eyes wide open

Snarl

Twitching
ear lobes

TALKING TO YOUR LAWYER ON THE TELEPHONE

Now and then, say once a year, you may feel you should talk to your attorney to see if he has news for you. Or, you may just want to keep in contact and check if your lawyer is still alive after all these years of handling your case.

Expect your first four or five phone calls to be ignored. You must understand that your lawyer has better things to do than to talk to his clients. Moreover, as he has told you on several occasions, he is not getting rich on your case. The thousands of dollars that you are paying him barely cover his expenses; he is toiling in your behalf practically pro bono. As likely or not, he will be at any or all of these locations at the time of your call: a) in court; b) in the Court of Appeals; c) in the United States Supreme Court.

Resist the temptation to have your lawyer paged at his country club in hopes of finding him. Lawyers resent such intrusions into their privacy. Remember that concentration is important to a golfer; you must not cause him to drive his next shot into the water. Besides, the price of a lost golf ball can be high and will probably show up on your next bill as "Miscellaneous Expenses."

Leave word in the office or on the answering machine, if at all possible. There is always a chance that he will return your call. If you don't hear back from your lawyer after six months, write him a letter. Then another. And still another. In due time, use a large manila envelope to accommodate any and all previous correspondence; if the envelope no longer holds, try a box.

Even if you get through, there is always the chance that your call will be cut short, probably in mid-sentence. Be appreciative of his time. Every minute counts, so keep it short. Stay away from asking such needless questions as:

- Has the case been put on the court calendar?
- Is the other party willing to settle?
- Has the court ruled in your favor?
- Has the court ruled against you?
- Any chance to appeal the decision?
- Has there been an order issued to sequester your home, your car or your bank account?

THE POWER OF POSITIVE TALKING

Experienced lawyers know the importance of keeping their clients' spirits high, whether or not there is reason for optimism. Happy clients pay their bills more willingly. A few well-chosen phrases can make all the difference.

WHEN LAWYERS SAY

IT MEANS

WHEN LAWYERS SAY	IT MEANS
At long last we can proceed with an appeal.	We lost the case in the lower court.
Congratulations! We made legal history today.	Judge gave opposing party highest award ever, setting a new legal precedent.

WHEN LAWYERS SAY | IT MEANS

WHEN LAWYERS SAY	IT MEANS
There will be a few minor expenses, of course.	There will be lots of major expenses.
Good news. We finally have a chance to relax for a while.	Another postponement was granted to the opposing party, the fifth one so far.
It's just a fishing expedition.	Opposing party has reasons to continue looking for additional evidence.
Our case has been put on the court calendar.	The case has a chance to come to trial in a year or two.
You will be able to repay your debt in no time at all.	Court order was issued to garnish your wages and attach your house.
We're standing firm.	Lawyer turned down a favorable offer for settlement.
Opposing lawyer called my office, but we're not going to respond.	The two lawyers have stopped talking to one another, eliminating any chances for a negotiated settlement.
I made my position clear and the judge listened very carefully.	Lawyer is held in contempt of court for his unprofessional conduct at trial.
It's just an opinion.	The court has issued a final judgment.
Don't worry about it.	Worry about it.

To make matters worse, lawyers use several words where one would suffice, in order to add weight to otherwise unweighty declarations.

LAWYERS AVOID	**LAWYERS USE**
as is	in its present condition
spouse	marriage partner
bill	statement of indebtedness
money	measure of value
marriage	conjugal union
mishap	injurious occurrence
gain	come into the possession of
share	divide proportionately

Redundancy also pays...and pays, and pays and pays. Like this:

LAWYERS USE	**INSTEAD OF**
Unless and Until	Unless
Null and Void	Void
Sum and Total	Total
Over and Above	Over
Each and Every	Each
By and between	Between

SUMMARY

1. Long words take up more space. This is why legal pads are a larger size than the regular kind.

2. Blue is the color used for legal covers. It puts the recipient in the right mood to read what's inside.

3. If lawyers could be understood by a layman, why hire one in the first place?

4. The concept of free speech is a strange one for a lawyer. He should have the right to charge his usual fee for speaking up.

5. Lawyers' favorite words are "whereas," "wherefore" and "for services rendered."

Chapter 5

It's Only Money—
Yours

A lawyer's favorite piece of writing is his monthly bill. Meticulous attention is paid to this document, more so than to any other document that leaves his desk.

It takes time to put all this lawyerly activity on paper, to verify every detail, confer with the accountants, computer operators, other record keepers and come up with just the right figure. Changes are frequent, particularly on timesheets suggesting the presence of less than twenty-five hour workdays, the very lowest number acceptable to the management of a law firm. Of course, there is always the possibility that the bill will be questioned by a client. Thank God for modern technology to help do away with this kind of argument. One may dispute a bill with a person but never with a computer.

Admittedly, it takes time to go over each and every itemized list but lawyers don't seem to mind. It goes with the service, they say. These explanations are the least they can do. Besides, drawing up a bill is a billable expense. Fair is fair.

Here's a typical scenario: You have just received a bill from your lawyer in the mail—all lawyers' bills arrive through the mail to avoid physical confrontation—and you decide to clear up a few minor points that caused you to go without sleep for the last three nights. You are particularly curious to find out the reason his monthly fee has more than tripled for no discernable reason.

Actually, doubts about his charges have crossed your mind many times before, but your sense of propriety prevented you from appearing overly inquisitive. After all, who are you to question the professional judgment of the very person you hired to represent you in a court of law? Not to mention the fact that your meddlesome prying may even lead you into potentially explosive areas, such as personal integrity. By now, you really should know your place. Hasn't counsel pointed out to you on not one but several occasions that your responsibility was to follow instructions and stay away from wasting his valuable time in discussing minutia, such as his billing?

However, it just so happens you have completed a four-week evening course on Personal Assertiveness. This seems to be as good a time as any to put your newly acquired skills to use, including—but not limited to—taking deep breaths and visualizing success.

So you pick up the phone. "I hate to quibble," you say, trying not to sound as if you are quibbling, "but I noticed on your bill..."

Your lawyer interrupts you. "I'm so glad you called," he shouts. His is a booming voice that shakes the receiver in your hand. "I was about to call you."

You feel much better now that he has told you that, considering that in all the years he represented you he never once took the initiative to contact you, save for pre-printed Christmas cards. As a result, your qualms about overstepping the bounds of good behavior may yet turn out to be the product of an overwrought mind.

"You were?" you ask.

"I was," he says. "Just to keep in touch with one of my favorite clients."

You are duly moved by his generous spirit and feel compelled to respond in kind. But his monthly bill stares you in the face and reality sets in. "Regarding some of the items..." you start out daringly.

"It's such a pleasure hearing from you," he roars. "And how are things with Murphy?" He is referring to your recent acquisition, a puppy of uncertain origin, including parts of a St. Bernard, a dachshund and a cocker spaniel. His name came up during the last chat with your lawyer when you were trying to make small talk to ease the moment.

"Murphy is doing fine, thank you very much."

"Is he housebroken yet?"

Oh yes, it's all coming back to you. The funny story you told him about Murphy's apparent inability to distinguish between table legs and fire hydrants. Your lawyer has a retentive mind; his talent for total recall must serve him in good stead in his work.

"He's beginning to get the message."

"Good," your lawyer proclaims. His voice drops to near normal level. "Dogs follow their noses," he waxes philosophically. "More so than their eyes. But they come around eventually, anyway. They are intelligent animals. All they need is a small dose of tender loving care as they learn. TLC." He laughs as if he has just told a joke.

But you refuse to be sidetracked. "To tell you the truth," you say, "I didn't call about Murphy. What I had in mind was to ask you a few questions about your last bill. All minor, of course."

"You mean our monthly statement," he corrects you. As any good lawyer will, yours, too, pays close attention to semantic distinctions. The term "bill" has yet to enter his vocabulary. It is probably too common a word, lacking the precision that is so important in everyday communication. It may be confused with legal paper money, a draft proposed for approval to a legislative body or the beak of a bird.

"Whatever. That is hardly the point..."

"I certainly have no objections to discussing our monthly statement with you. Or with any of my clients, for that matter. If only you hadn't caught me at this particular time. We're just getting ready for a conference, gathering up material. And if there is one thing I detest, it is to cut anyone short, I myself would find that offensive, as I am sure you would, too."

"This will only take a minute... if we could just clear up a few points that confuse me..."

"Confuse?"

"Well, caught my attention, if you will. Your itemized breakdown indicates twenty-two phone calls in the last thirty days, all lasting exactly a half hour. No more, no less."

Your lawyer is not about to lose his cool. "My secretary keeps tabs of all the calls, and it's our policy to round up all the numbers. It simplifies our bookkeeping, as I am sure you can understand."

There is a pause. You take a deep breath. "And I couldn't help noticing," you go on evenly, "that nineteen of the calls were made between your office and opposing counsel. Perhaps my memory fails to serve me right, but didn't you tell me last month that she would be on vacation for at least six weeks?"

"I might have mentioned that to you. Of course, that doesn't mean that we would stop your case from proceeding business as usual—that would be a disservice to you. Her office and ours have an understanding that in the event of absence of principals, our associates pick up the pieces. I hope you appreciate that."

"But didn't you also state that for all practical purposes the court holds a recess during the summer months, particularly with the judge on vacation? I am not sure, of course, and it is far from my intention to imply..."

"The wheels of justice may slow down but they never come to a halt. That is not the way our justice systems works. It would run squarely against the principles of due process, the principles on which our society rests. So we just keep hammering away on your case, no matter what the circumstances. As reflected on our monthly statement, I believe."

Your eyes scan the bill again and again, growing watery along the way. "Perhaps it is my inexperience," you say, "but I have difficulty identifying the nature of every call. All I see is my name versus the opposition."

"Precisely. And that is all we need."

You pause to gather your thoughts, which seem to scatter in every direction. You are, you decide, at a complete loss. Which proves again that when it comes to legal matters, you would be better off leaving them in the hands of an expert. But you refuse to listen to your better judgment and go on. "Another thing," you say. "Fifty-two hours for research? Isn't that a bit on...well, on the high side? I mean based on your past observations regarding this case."

"What observations?"

"That the issues involved here were rather simple and familiar to you. A classic textbook situation, I believe, was the way you put it."

His voice changes from frosty to freezing. "That might be so. Which is the reason why we work on your case far below our usual rates."

Numbers dance inside your head. Calculator in hand, you quickly tote up the hours appearing on the bill. It occurs to you that based on his time sheets, your lawyer must be over 100 years old. He certainly doesn't show his age; here you were, thinking he was in his forties.

"The question I have is simple," you say. "Why is so much time spent on research on a case that you described as routine?"

Your lawyer is losing his patience. "Nobody ever said litigation was cheap." But now his tone changes to conciliatory, "Let us look at this situation in the long range. Consider the costs as a future investment."

You perk up at the words future investment. "Am I to understand that you are confident that we can win this case and recoup the costs?"

"Well, there is always that possibility." He laughs. "Judges are human beings, after all, too. As such they are prone to mood changes. Not to mention, personal predilections and biases. No telling what they do. In this business, the only certainty is uncertainty. But that is hardly the real issue here."

"Just what is the real issue then?"

"Your feelings. Think about it. What's more important to you? A dollar here, a dollar there? Or your peace of mind?"

SUMMARY

1. Who says lawyers lack imagination? Their monthly bills are creative masterpieces.

2. No lawyer has ever been accused of lack of diligence when it comes to collecting his own fees.

3. Remember, you are paying for preparation. Like preparing your next monthly bill.

4. Lawyers have often been compared to sharks. That is an insult...to the sharks.

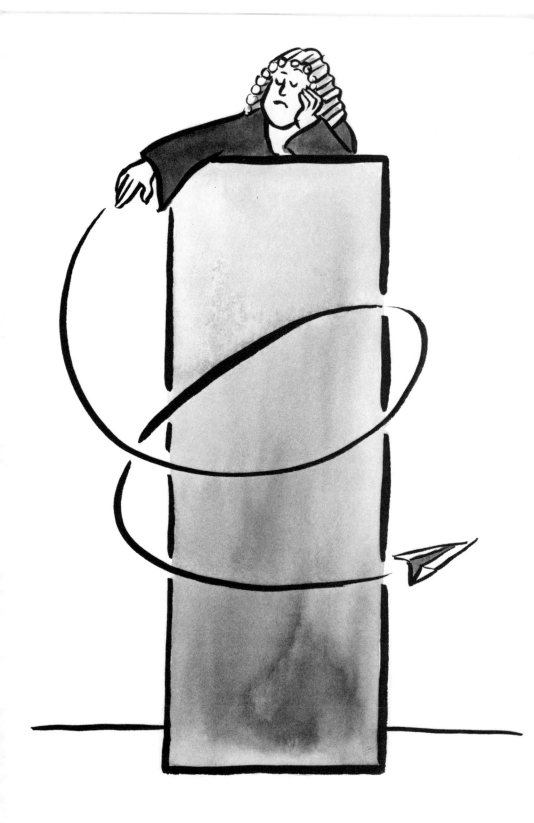

Chapter 6

See You in Court

NO lawyer will admit that he actually enjoys going to court. The very thought seems to fill him with consternation.

"You don't want to go to court," he will tell you as if the choice were yours.

"And why not?" you ask.

His answer borders on cryptic. "That's the last place you want to be," he says.

You wonder why. It has been your impression that under the American system of jurisprudence this is where people go to resolve their legal differences. It is here that lawyers can argue their cases before an administrator of justice, pro and con, and as loudly as their diaphragms allow them to do so.

But no, you are wrong again. Your lawyer shakes his head at your incredible naivete. "Our court system," he explains with patience usually reserved for a young pupil trying to catch up with the rest of the class, "is not for the civilized world." He pauses to allow his statement to sink deeply into your conscience. "The system," he then continues, using his favorite word again, "is slow, inefficient and onerous to the extreme. Judges dictate the pace. Not us, time-conscious lawyers. It can take months, even years, for a case to even be called." He gives you one of his toothy smiles. "If ever."

You're not smiling. Based on his remarks, you are about to let go of the case, walk away from the whole thing. "Not to mention the money part," he goes on still grinning. "Look at it this way. My job, as your attorney, is to save you expenses, right? Well, dragging your case through the system can cost you a small fortune, if you know what I mean."

You know exactly what he means. "Small fortune" in the jargon of the profession means a "large fortune."

Motion to dismiss motion to... interlocutory motion...

"So I believe it is my duty to advise you as your counsel to forget about going to court. Let us not be foolish." He then proceeds to litigate your case in the court of law. One motion follows the next. You have a hard time following the proceedings; like a patient under multiple medications, even the names of motions leave you in a state of bewilderment. Vaguely you recall there have been alternative motions, ex parte motions, interlocutory motions, motions for more definite statements, motions for a trial, motions for a nonsuit, motions for a decree, motions to dismiss, motions for summary judgment, motions for judgment notwithstanding, motions for reargument, motions to squash, motions to set aside judgment, motions to vacate judgment, motions to strike, premature motions, revival of motions, omnibus motions and, finally, a motion to withdraw all motions.

All the while your lawyer complains about his deteriorating physical and mental well-being, what with all the goings-on. He complains about having to go to court to submit a motion, complains after having submitted it and complains about waiting for motions yet to be decided. Clearly, you are causing him pain, a pathological condition. Some of the inflictions that still befall him he has never experienced before, among them chronic fatigue syndrome, acidosis and herpes zoster.

You fully expect to see a medical bill attached to his next regular monthly statement under "Miscellaneous Expenses."

The fact is that lawyers enjoy going to court. They have every reason to. For one thing, the trip to the place of adjudication gives them a chance to get out of the office. A chance they haven't had since, say, yesterday. They now have an opportunity to be among friends, their own peers who understand them and will trade gossip about new job opportunities. The place is furnished for their maximum body comfort and peace of mind. All rooms—the courtroom, the judge's chambers, the bathroom stalls—offer cozy seating arrangements, an opportunity for the lawyer to catch up on his reading and sleep. If there are elevators in the building, they are built to move in slow motion, about a foot a minute; this is to give lawyers and judges an opportunity to exchange pleasantries and find out how each other's families are doing. Most importantly, there are clocks in nearly every courtroom, put there to remind lawyers that all is not lost; as time ticks away, they become richer by the hour, if not by the minute.

A lawyer's application for postponement will surprise no one, least of all the judge who himself frequently took the same route in his days as a practicing attorney. Nor is it likely that the opposing counsel will raise objections; he expects the same treatment—laughingly described as "professional courtesy" in the trade—when it is his turn to ask for yet another postponement.

Such mutual trust between opposing forces is not only heartwarming but also practical for all those concerned. It does away with complicated excuses when asking for deferment. These will do:

Over-anxious clients may insist on more detailed reasons for the wait. No need to fret. The legal profession has a long list of alibis designed to set their minds at ease:

I'm working on it.

We're playing for time.

Yours is a complex case.

Gotta do our homework first.

We're networking it.

It's in the computer.

Lost the disc.

The FAX machine broke down.

I'm sorry... who is this...?

WHEN IN DOUBT, ASK FOR PRE-TRIAL DISCOVERIES

In preparing for a trial, judges happily grant either or both lawyers an order for discovery proceedings—an opportunity for both parties to obtain real or imagined evidence to prepare their cases before trial. The idea is to make the judge's life easier, if not the litigant's.

Lawyers approve of the concept. Here at long last is an opportunity to combine the court's interest with their own. The technique can keep the case from reaching trial for weeks, months—and in the hands of competent counsel—years.

I'll take two pre-trial discoveries, one postponement, and ¼ lb. Brie.

There are many ways to make sure discovery proceedings do not end abruptly say, less than a day for each meeting. Witnesses can be summoned to appear; if they are nowhere to be found, another date can be set. Requests can be made to produce documents. In the event of refusal, a motion to compel can be set in motion which can be challenged in a separate action which takes time to decide and which can then again be challenged.

Depositions are usually held in the office of one of the lawyers; a conference room complete with comfortable armchairs will do just fine. The atmosphere is informal, with participants free to speak their minds. By far the most important person in the room is the court reporter. It is his job to take down anything being said, including obscenities, profanities and all the jokes told, funny or not. He gets paid by the word, not by the hour.

SUMMARY

1. Due process was invented by lawyers for lawyers to make sure that in the legal process they get paid what is due them.

2. Postponement gives a lawyer enough time to prepare a new motion to ask the court for another postponement.

3. The term "motion" is a misnomer.

4. Taking oaths is part of Discovery Proceedings. Most oaths are four-letter words.

Chapter 7

Yes, We Do Divorces

HAVING searched your souls for many months, you and your spouse finally conclude that it would be best for both of you to end your marriage. You have talked things over and arrived at what appears to be a fair settlement. In fact, for quite some time both of you have been busy striking up new friendships with an eye towards future happiness.

It has occurred to you, in fact, that in view of the success of a negotiated settlement and absence of rancor there was no reason for you not to have the same lawyer—your "family" lawyer—formalize the agreement. A few simple boilerplate documents will be all you need, plain logic tells you.

Seated in your respective chairs across his desk, your mutually agreed upon lawyer's eyes travel back and forth between the two of you as if he were watching a tennis game. "Any chance of you two getting together again?" he finally asks.

You shake your heads in unison and ask him why he wants to know. "We always feel that our clients should be asked this question," he says.

"Emotions run deep in cases like this and if there is any chance for reconciliation between parties, this is the time to find out. Policy, you know. Contrary to what you may think, we don't particularly enjoy seeing marriages fail. We're all human beings, after all, first and foremost."

You tell him that you passed the marriage counseling stage some time ago.

He shuffles papers from one stack on his desk to another, and back again while reflecting upon your statement. "Well then," he says resignedly, "we have no choice but to set things in motion. Here's the first step. One of you will have to engage the services of another attorney to represent you."

The news sets you aback just a little. You have worked everything out between yourselves you tell him: child support, division of property, ownership of the car, the television sets, the dog's visitation rights. It's all on paper neatly typed, signed and notarized.

The lawyer examines the documents you drew up and frowns. "I admire the time and effort you spent on formalizing your understanding," he says in due course. "As a matter of fact, I must commend you. Unfortunately, I cannot as an attorney tell you that these instruments in their present form will stand up in court."

"And why not?"

"Please, don't misunderstand me. I'm not suggesting the judge will not take a good look at them. Of course he will. But remember, it behooves the court to go beyond good intentions. Terminating a marriage is a serious matter and I see a number of grey areas in your agreement."

"Grey areas?" you ask.

"Lack of fair disclosure, misrepresentation, misunderstandings between parties, just to mention a few possibilities. And the judge will certainly want to know the type of representation either of you has received. Sharing the same attorney could be one of the problems that might be considered sticky."

The lawyer savors the impact of his words before he goes on. "But as I said earlier, I would be happy to represent either of you. Far from me to choose sides."

You flip a coin; call heads or tails. Wife stays with the lawyer; husband exits.

"Oh, yes," the attorney says, but adds reassuringly, "I know just how you feel and I don't blame you. I, too, want to get this case over as quickly as possible. I'm with you all the way."

A few days later, she (plaintiff) reads a copy of the Divorce Complaint against her husband (defendant) and promptly calls her lawyer for an appointment.

"I don't understand," she tells him in his office, her voice breaking. "I told you my husband and I have already come to an agreement. We are both prepared to call it quits, perhaps remarry again soon. Why include eight different grounds for a divorce in our Complaint at this stage of the game?"

The lawyer's face melts into a smile. "I guess that's why you and millions of others like you need legal advice. It's up to us to keep our clients from making mistakes and then having to pay for them for the rest of their natural lives." He continues. "Let me tell you something about judges. They're people, too, like you and me. Many are married and know only too well what it's like to live under the same roof with the same person, day in and day out, argue and make up. It's only natural for them to look at the conduct of both parties, the total picture."

"But it says here that my husband drank habitually. He did no such thing. If anyone should know, I should."

"Are you telling me he never touched the stuff?"

"A beer or two, perhaps, a few sips of white wine. That's about it. Hardly the qualifications to be granted lifelong membership in Alcoholics Anonymous."

"Has his mood ever changed under the influence?"

"He'd loosen up a bit, of course. Like anyone else. That's the whole idea, isn't it?"

"Did he ever show signs of aggressive behavior during his drinking sprees?"

"Well, he'd let go a few jokes, perhaps..."

"Off color, perhaps?"

"Not in my presence he wouldn't. His biggest problem was that he'd repeat the same jokes over and over again. But

that does not constitute grounds for divorce, does it now?"

"Has anyone ever been privy to his unusual behavior as you have just described it?"

"I am sure there must have been quite a few people. We've had many friends and he appreciated an audience."

"So if need be, we can call on witnesses to testify. That's good."

She has a problem sharing his enthusiasm and maintains her fix on the copy of the Divorce Complaint in her hands. The strain of trying to absorb her husband's long list of wrongdoings begins to have its effect. She points at another paragraph, this, too, referenced by a number. "What is the word 'non-support' supposed to mean anyway? And here, 'gross neglect'? You can't be serious."

"Those terms are quite explicit in their legal implications, my good lady. They simply point to your husband's reluctance to provide support for you and your family. Based on his income, of course."

"But it wouldn't be fair to accuse him of that. As a matter of fact, if anything, he is a rather generous person."

"Are you saying he has never once refused to respond to your needs?"

" 'Needs,' is too strong a word, I would think. 'Wants,' would be more like it. It would have been nice to have a third car in the family, for example."

"Means of transportation could be construed as a necessity. Tell me, what would have been the purpose of having a third car in the family?"

"Our oldest son was nearing driving age. He wanted to get his wheels, he insisted, to improve his social standing. The two cars we had were in constant use. One by my husband, one by myself, mostly to drive our youngest to school and do some shopping. One more car would have been a Godsend under the circumstances."

The lawyer exclaims, "You see, there we are. Get the point? Another vehicle would have been more than just a luxury item. In point of fact, it was an essential for your family's well-being."

He proceeds to read aloud the rest of the allegations tallied up in the Complaint. Mental cruelty, he explains to his client apparently ignorant of her rights under the law, is based on the insults he would hurl at her in the heat of an argument in front of others, specifically on one occasion at a husband/wife golf tournament, when he suggested that she take lessons on getting out of sandtraps. Twice he overlooked their wedding anniversary, and he was prone to working late in the office for reasons less than clear.

"Are you accusing my husband of being unfaithful, too?" the wife asks. "That's a new one on me."

"We live in a less than perfect world," the lawyer says. "We would be remiss not to suggest the possibility of extramarital relations in a divorce complaint. We may not be able to prove anything, but it's worth a try. Now let's get down to the heart of the matter, shall we? Where are you going to live?"

"We agreed that I would keep the house until such time as the children leave home. We both will continue to pay the mortgage and then divide the money from the sale between us."

"What about the standard of living to which you are accustomed?"

"My plan is to accept a part time job that will help to cover expenses. We agreed on the amount of child support payments and all that. And there will be enough money set aside for the children's college education."

"Have you been looking for employment yet?"

"I already received a few offers. I am among the lucky ones with a good education and practical working experience."

The lawyer holds up his hand as if trying to stop the rush of oncoming traffic. "Now let's not get carried away too early by your professional qualifications. The operative word is caution. I am firmly against your accepting a job before the trial. Your proven ability to earn a living may count heavily against us in deciding on the amount of monthly alimony and child support payments."

She objects, "Listen, I don't want to wear down my husband. God knows, he tried. And frankly, I don't want to depend on his monthly stipends either."

The lawyer sinks into an even deeper gloom. "Just what do you have in mind?" he asks. "There is no way I will allow your husband to take advantage of you like that. You're asking me to give the store away after all these years you invested in being a good wife, a good mother."

"He has been a good husband, and a good father, too."

The lawyer refuses to permit himself to be distracted by details less than pertinent. "Surely, he owes you something for all the sacrifices you made in his behalf during the best part of your life."

More documents wrapped in legal blue reach the wife a few days later. She reads them with more than passing interest. They are signed by her soon-to-be ex-husband.

"Did you see the papers?" she pants in her lawyer's office.

"Of course, I have," the lawyer says. "They represent your husband's General Denial and Counterclaim. You seem upset."

"I never thought my husband would stoop as low as this," the wife says, her eyes moist with tears.

The lawyer assumes his avuncular posture. "Your husband's attorney did exactly what he was supposed to do. He submitted a cross motion. It's to be expected. Remember, this is an adversary situation."

The wife reads from the document. "He contends I was mentally and physically abusive, that I failed to perform my wifely duties, that I willfully stood in the way of his career, that I neglected the children, that I belittled him in front of his boss at a dinner party.

And, oh yes, that I regularly consorted with other men while still married."

"Well, did you?"

"Not while we both still were committed to maintaining our marriage. Things have changed, of course, in the last six months or so. We came to a mutual understanding as to our personal aspirations. Both of us began to look for new friends."

The lawyer clears his throat. "These so-called friends of yours... Have you ever spent time with them...uh, in their homes?"

"A few times, perhaps. I couldn't very well invite them to my house, not with my kids and my husband still living there."

The lawyer makes notes on a yellow pad. He looks up at long last.

"I certainly hope that you are prepared to put a stop to all that as of right now."

"I'm not sure if I get your point."

"I would think you understand that the court may have a few reservations about your going out on dates while still married."

"What about my husband? He doesn't spend his evenings all by his lonesome. I know he doesn't. And to be honest, I perfectly understand why he wouldn't."

"The judge may not agree with your position," the lawyer says opening and searching through his desk drawer while talking. He finds a business card and holds it up. "As a matter of fact, I'm glad you brought up the subject. Obviously, we have our work cut out for us. I want you to look up this fellow. I highly recommend him. He delivers."

"Delivers what?" The wife lets out a nervous laugh. "Laundry? Chinese food?"

"It's incumbent upon us," the lawyer goes on, ignoring the interruption, "that we put your husband under close surveillance. "Maybe we'll be able to drop a bombshell or two at the divorce hearing, eh?"

The wife meets with the private investigator so highly praised by the lawyer. He comes complete with a wristwatch that tells everything but the time, a recording system that fills his briefcase and a fountain pen that also acts as a flashlight.

"Will you really be needing all this?" she asks.

He enjoys her surprise at his paraphernalia and points with pride to his paneled delivery truck marked Drop Dead Pest Control. "This ain't no 'Good Humor' bottle popper," he explains. "We're talking parabolic and shotgun mikes, ultraviolet video cameras, and telephone listening devices here. Madam, your husband is a goner."

"Now wait a minute. I think we should discuss..."

"You will receive from us a daily journal covering all his movements," he says reassuringly. "Time and place—broken down minute by minute."

The itemized lists issued by Drop Dead Pest Control are exactly as promised. There are detailed accounts of the husband's activities. She learns about his favorite restaurants, the food he ordered and the time it took him to finish his meals, his dates, his phone conversations and much more that she had long been familiar with.

"We're making progress," the lawyer says gleefully as he examines the reports.

The judge is less impressed. He glances frequently at his watch, and he tells both attorneys the court wishes to limit the divorce trial to the finances of the parties.

The hearing itself takes less than an hour with the judge reading the terms of the couple's original agreement into the record. He congratulates the litigants on their ability to handle their problems in such mature fashion. The lawyers shake their clients' hands as they pack up to leave the courtroom, each proclaiming victory.

"My dear," the wife's attorney says to her, "as of this very minute you are a free woman. Now if there is anything...anything at all I can do for you, just let me know. I am still your counsel, and hope a good friend as well."

"I think I'll just go around the corner and get myself a cup of coffee. Call it a celebration, if you like." She doesn't know whether to smile or cry.

"A wonderful idea," the lawyer says, agreeing with his client for the first time in two years. "I know just the place." He mentions a midtown restaurant famous for its haute cuisine, and equally haute prices.

He tells her between the entree and dessert, "You have been an exceptional client. It must have been an emotional drain for you to deal with someone like your husband. But as we like to say, it is the results that count. We might have lost a battle or two but we won the war."

He lifts his cup of espresso at the end of a long luncheon. "Here's to a happy and prosperous future."

The waiter now brings a cordless telephone to the table. It seems the lawyer has an urgent call from his office. "Emergency," he says as he stands up and hurries out the door.

She picks up the tab.

SUMMARY

1. To a divorce lawyer happiness is finding an unhappy marriage.

2. Divorce lawyers heartily approve of marriage. Without it, they would be out of business.

3. The most common cause for getting a divorce is marriage.

4. Equitable distribution is when the divorced couple gets half the assets and the lawyer gets the other half.

Chapter 8

The Company Lawyer: It's a Living

I N the life of any business organization, in-house counsel plays an important, if not indispensable, role. Just ask any in-house counsel. It should be kept in mind that his professional legal advice is an essential part in the foundation of a business entity. It is he who assists the founders in structuring the organization, to say nothing of the design of corporate stationery, both letter and envelope. Moreover, he oversees the distribution of stock, making sure everyone gets his fair share (including himself), and, of course, the election of officers (assuring his rightful seat on the board).

Having done that, he can now address himself to the solutions of the myriad legal problems that become part of doing everyday business. He keeps the company from making grievous mistakes and, finally, he is on hand as it goes into bankruptcy, with top management facing choices of filing for Chapters 7, 11, 13 or simply leaving town.

This is not to suggest that between the birth of the corporation and bankruptcy of same, his finely honed skills are not in constant demand.

For example, he is in the best of all positions to explain the corporate charter to the founders who yet do not understand a word of it. This achievement alone should more than justify his two-to-six window office, plus the services of a legal secretary who can tell him what it is he is supposed to do next.

With so much on the agenda, company in-house lawyers have little time to spare. The pressure is unrelenting; it is fair to say that like all lawyers, they more than earn their keep. This would be their typical day:

A LAWYER'S DAY

9:45-10:00 A.M.	Arrives in the office, scans *The Wall Street Journal*, studies the *Help Wanted Classified* ads at length.
10:01 A.M.	His coffee is served. He wants more cream.
10:03 A.M.	His secretary pours more cream in his coffee.
10:20 A.M.	He wants to know whether he has received any important calls this morning, or unimportant ones, for that matter.
10:21 A.M.	He is told that the Financial Vice President of the corporation called to confirm their lunch appointment. Lawyer suggests to make it a half hour later on account of his heavy schedule.
10:30-11:30 A.M.	Lawyer looks at documents taken from the incoming box, including a list of bonuses about to be distributed to key executives in the company; himself included. He goes over the script of an upcoming television commercial submitted by the company's advertising agency for his legal approval.

11:46 A.M.-12:30 P.M.	He dictates a five-page memo in response to a memo sent to his office on the subject of excessively long memos.
12:30-12:50 P.M.	Lawyer looks out the window. Looking down fills him with a sense of power. Looking up puts him in direct touch with God.
1:00-3:15 P.M.	He has lunch in the executive dining room with the Financial Vice President who wants to discuss his daughter's legal position as to getting her landlord to fix the plumbing in the bathroom. They drink to that.
3:16-3:20 P.M.	Members of the advertising agency are waiting for him in the reception area as he returns, slightly unsteady on his feet. The agency account executive helps him to stay in an upright position as they walk toward the conference room.
3:22 P.M.	Counsel apologizes for being late due to his workload. "You know how it is," he smiles. Everyone around the table nods.
3:40 P.M.	Counsel holds up television storyboard and scowls.
3:41-3:45 P.M.	Everyone else scowls.
3:46-3:48 P.M.	Lawyer puts storyboard back on the table and stands up. Managing to keep his balance, he looks around the room.
3:49 P.M.	"Excuse me," he says finally. "I'll be back shortly." Everyone nods. Counsel says: "I will take this under advisement while away." He heads for the bathroom with storyboard under his arm.

4:25 P.M..	Counsel returns. "Well, what do you think?" the account executive asks. Counsel grins. Beads of sweat appear on the account executive's forehead as he waits. The creative director stares at the ceiling. The art director clutches his head.
5:06 P.M.	"I like it," counsel says at long last. There is a collective sigh. "It's a fine commercial," the account executive says, "Everyone in the agency thinks so." "I have no problem with it," counsel says. "But to make sure, I'd like to think about it for a few days, if you don't mind."
5:20-5:30 P.M.	He returns to his office, calls his broker and tells him about his company's impending leveraged buyout, and instructs him to purchase more stock in same.
5:31-6:00 P.M.	He fills out a timesheet showing hours spent on corporate matters.

High in management, corporate lawyers are often asked to make far-reaching decisions. Few could be considered "Yes Men." Words like "No," "Naw," "Forget it" and "Over my dead body," flow more naturally from their lips than an affirmative vote. Their value to the corporation, in fact—and they would be the first to agree—lies in their courage to say "no" and effectively halt projects before the damage is done. Studies show corporate lawyers wear shirts with a neck size two above average as a result of shaking their heads from side-to-side through their years of service.

Those with experience offer opinions only when asked. For the most part, they will resist putting anything on paper. Should they have no alternative, they will do their professional best to avoid even the slightest hint of a final conclusion which may yet come back to haunt them.

HOW LAWYERS AVOID GIVING OPINIONS

1. Offer a minimum of six solutions to every problem, covering every angle. Make frequent use of words like "and/or," "either/or," and "whether or not."

2. Qualify every statement. Key phrases are: "perhaps," "as the case may be," "if at all."

3. Avoid use of "it will be," "likely," "I believe."

4. Use initials in place of a full name, especially if they happen to be identical to others in the organization.

5. Distribute the memo to everyone in the office, including the shipping clerk who just arrived from Russia and has yet to learn the language. Names of recipients appear on top of first page to show the number of people sharing exactly the same information.

6. Refer to this memo as a "personal opinion."

SUMMARY

1 The best way to avoid a problem is not to bring it up at all.

2. The best way to avoid product liability is to stop the product from being produced at all.

3. The word "no" is shorter than "yes."

4. When in doubt, ask your secretary.

Chapter 9

No Pain, No Gain

O F all the practitioners of law, personal injury lawyers are the proudest of their mission; it is they who see to it that their clients get compensated for pain and suffering, hospital stays, medical attention, psychological harm, and, most importantly, for legal services.

It goes without saying, heartfelt compassion plays an important role in their kind of work. As often as not, a personal injury lawyer will refuse to accept any and all payment for his services until such time that the court determines the size of the award. Even then, most personal injury lawyers allow their clients to keep what is left, after payment of legal fees and sundry expenses—provided there is anything left.

No other type of lawyer cares as deeply about the health and happiness of his fellow beings as does this lawyer. His heart is in the right place. He is there when needed, arriving moments after, or sometimes even before the accident, ready to lend a helping hand. He will wait for the ambulance to arrive at the hospital; follow his client's gurney all the way to the operating room; pay frequent visits to his bedside bearing flowers, a tape recorder and camcorder; and attend his funeral service with a briefcase in hand.

In the aftermath of an accident, he may yet turn out to be his client's best friend. He not only understands; he understands more than you'd ever thought possible.

Suppose one evening you trip on the sidewalk on your way home from the office. A minor annoyance, to be sure, but you're the conservative type who likes to make sure. So you go and see your friendly podiatrist the very next day after the accident.

The man in the white coat rotates your ankle forward, backwards and sideways in his office as his nurse watches, ready to provide artificial resuscitation in case you lose consciousness. He wiggles your big toe. "Feel anything?" he asks at long last.

You admit that you are aware of his ministrations. Still, you're determined not to overreact. "I'm all right, Doc," you reassure him. "Particularly if you'd only stop whatever it is that you're doing."

He refuses to take no for an answer. "Most likely the problem is your metatarsal bone," he says. "Second digit to be exact." He asks his nurse to take you into the next room for a few X-ray pictures. He slaps the transparencies against his light box upon receiving them and studies them at length.

"Anything serious?" you ask.

Your podiatrist smiles reassuringly. "Nothing nature can't fix. Take it easy for a day or two and everything will turn out just fine." You put your shoes back on and leave the office with the nurse leading the way.

The next day you get a call from an attorney you never even heard of. He tells you his office specializes in compensable injury cases such as yours. And that's not all. He represented doctors, hospitals and insurance companies at the beginning of his career, taking on both plaintiffs and defendants. But then he saw the light. His sense of justice got the better of him. Today he is on the side of the victims.

You tell him yours was an accident hardly worth all the attention. You are not in pain, never have been and probably never will be.

He is not easily swayed, however. "No accident is too small for us," he responds immediately. "You have suffered bodily and emotional harm and are entitled to just compensation. So says the law. Let us get together soon at our mutual convenience. Provided you're ambulatory, of course. If not, I'll be happy to visit you at home."

Anyone erudite enough to use words like "ambulatory" deserves attention. Your curiosity piqued, you agree to go and meet the caller.

His office is decorated to set the injured party's mind at ease. Hanging on the wall are large medical diagrams of various parts of the anatomy: the skull, the chest, the hip, the arms and finally, the legs. Red predominates, the color of blood. He catches you looking at the pictures.

"Our body is a truly amazing phenomenon," he says, as you look at the pictures with awe. "Don't you think so?"

"I certainly do."

"But it is also a delicate, complex mechanism," he goes on. "Lots of things can go wrong with it. Now, let's talk about you. How come you're not on crutches?"

"I don't need them."

He walks around his desk to help you sit down. "You're okay?" he asks.

"Couldn't be better."

"I don't think you realize the seriousness of your injury," he says.

"I'm not in pain. I think I should tell you that I have a golf date this Sunday and I don't intend to miss it. There's no way I'll let my buddies tee off without me."

He is not convinced. "C'mon now," he tells you peremptorily. "You are in pain. You understand my point? Listen to what I have to say. I think we can make this thing stick. But not without your cooperation. For starters, we'll notify your employer that you'll be staying home for two weeks on account of your injury. Our office will supply you with a pair of crutches when you leave, so you will be able to hobble out of here in an appropriate manner. And I want you to stay on those crutches until after the trial."

"But why? I can make my way without them."

"Don't try to be a hero, you hear? I've got your medical report right

1.   2.   3.

in front of me. Your podiatrist's nurse was nice enough to send me copies of your diagnosis, X-rays and all the documentation we need. Now let me ask you a few questions about your accident. Did anyone see you fall down?"

"I didn't fall. I stumbled, got up and went on my way."

"You fell. Now, just where exactly did the accident take place?"

"In front of the building at the corner of Northern Avenue and Brooks Street."

"What brought you there?"

"I was on my way home from the office."

"So it was rather late in the day?"

"Yes."

"And the visibility was poor, right? The street lights didn't work?"

"I don't remember."

"Oh yes, you do. The street lights didn't work. A city responsibility. What was the weather like?"

"Cloudy. It snowed most of the afternoon."

"Was the sidewalk clear of snow?"

"It must have been, I guess."

"Did you see anyone removing the snow? Scraping off the ice?"

"Not while I was there."

"No wonder you fell. The owner of the building failed to keep the

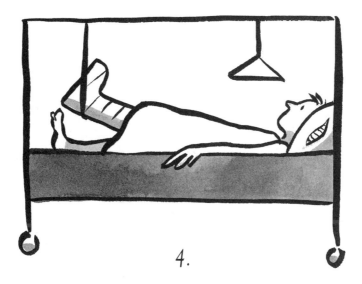

4.

(1) Upon your arrival at the lawyer's office, your pain is minimal and basically ignored. (2) But with your first filing of papers against the defendant(s), crutches are necessary for overall effect. (3) Wheelchairs are imperative when consulting opposing counsel and (4) on the day of the trial, an adjustable hospital bed assures you a court victory.

ground in front of his property safe enough for pedestrian traffic, a classic case of actionable negligence. What were you wearing at the time of the accident?"

"An overcoat, a business suit..."

"I mean on your feet."

"A pair of shoes. My brown oxfords, if I recall."

"Your footwear may also have played a part in your losing your balance. There could be a case of product liability here. Looking better all the time. Anything else you can think of?"

"Not much else. Except...I did have my usual at the bar on my way home. A few beers."

"Good. A bartender served them to you. And then, to make matters worse, he permitted you to leave the premises in an inebriated state, didn't hail a taxi, ask anyone to escort you home or even offer you a cup of coffee before letting you go outside to fight the snowstorm."

"Well..."

"Perfect. What we have here are four defendants so far. The city, the owner of the building, the footwear manufacturer and the bartender."

SUMMARY

1. It's no longer true that lawyers chase ambulances. They're at the hospital waiting for ambulances to arrive.

2. Personal injury lawyers work under great pressure. There is always a chance that their client may pass away before trial.

3. Victims may experience great emotional distress following an accident. They always experience greater emotional distress when they see their lawyer's bill.

4. A personal injury lawyer's favorite animal is a vicious dog.

5. A personal injury lawyer's favorite places are chemical dumping grounds, busy highway intersections and nuclear reactor plants.

Chapter 10

Here Comes the Judge!

t is the judge who hands down the final decision. This arrangement suits lawyers just fine. Should the case go against their client, they can blame the court. On the other hand, they can take full credit for a favorable ruling.

Rarely do lawyers act surprised at the outcome of a trial; as you would expect from a professional, they take things in stride. If asked, they can be quite vocal about what has gone wrong. To hear them tell it, adverse determinations of the court have little if anything to do with the presentation of the case or fine points of the law. More than likely, the problem began with the judge's own deep-seated personality conflicts going back to his early childhood. Superiority complex, manic depression, multiple personality disorders, delusionary visions and low intelligence quotient are just some of the symptoms. Such aberrations may escape the attention of a layman, but not learned counsel who faces the judge.

Everything about his honor appears to be designed to intimidate those standing before him. He sits on a platform several feet above floor level, so that he can look down at the world-at-large, more specifically at lawyers arguing their cases. He wears a loose, billowing robe that hides his crumpled suits, wrinkled shirts and protruding belly. His arrival is greeted with a resounding, "Hear ye, hear ye," as spectators jump to attention like raw recruits in boot camp. Nothing of the kind awaits the lawyer.

Ask your attorney to describe the personality of the judge presiding over your case and he will tell you your chances for winning are all but nonexistent—unless, of course, he can save the day by way of his superior presentation. Chances are the judge in question will fit one or more of the following descriptions.

TYPES OF JUDGES

THE EFFICIENCY EXPERT is eager to move on. He bears built-in hostility towards all lawyers who, in his opinion, are the sole cause for the backlog on his calendar.

THE STORYTELLER is never at a loss for personal anecdotes, real or fancied. His jokes may be on the stale side, but not to his ever-changing audience in the courtroom.

THE SIDEBAR RULER is given to motioning counsels to approach the bench. He leans across the desk as he chides them. His favorite question, loud enough for everyone to hear, is "Counsel, just what is it you have in mind?"

THE DIPLOMAT prefers his chambers to the courtroom. Surrounded by his books and mementos, he can relax here and tell both sides just what he has in mind in the way of settling the case. Anyone ignoring his suggestions does so at his own peril.

THE PERFECTIONIST goes by the book, his book. He is familiar with his precedents and cites them often. Pity the lawyer facing this judge.

THE OGRE says very little as he reigns over the case. There is no way of knowing which side he is on, if any.

SUMMARY

1. The reason why so many judges feel lawyers waste their time is that lawyers do waste their time.

2. Judges tend to suspect lawyers. They used to be lawyers themselves.

3. Judges like to don their black robes. It symbolizes authority and adds a nice funereal touch to the proceedings.

4. The length of a court recess often depends on the distance between the bench and the bathroom.

Chapter 11

Who Can You Call?

Even in the face of possibilities, you may find yourself looking for the one attorney you feel can handle your case. Chances are your friends and relatives can help you. They probably have had their own encounters with counsel; the fact that they are able to live and tell about it is a good sign.

Perhaps you yourself already know someone in the field. It is perfectly all right to ask that person for a recommendation. He will suggest the best he knows: None other than himself. Your problem is solved.

A professional referral service can also point you in the right direction. For a reasonable fee, such an organization will recommend another organization which for a reasonable fee will recommend still another organization which will for a reasonable fee recommend a lawyer who may or may not be able to handle your case.

Moreover, you may consult your classified telephone directory for names of lawyers in your area. The list appears in the "L" section, usually between Lawn Mowers and Lemon Juices, an interesting coincidence.

Of course, you may ask: Do I need a lawyer at all? This is an important question, the kind you should never bring up in the presence of a lawyer if you want to keep him as a friend. The fact is that disputes can often be settled outside the court. Suppose someone punches you in the nose. You can always punch him back. If he is bigger than you are, that's another story. In that case, you just may need a lawyer.

Generally speaking, you will feel more comfortable having a lawyer on your side once the case goes to court. A lawyer is more familiar with the surroundings and with the way business is conducted. He may yet save you from the embarrassment of confusing the clerk of the court with the presiding judge, the jury box with the benches for the general public and the judge's chamber with the bathroom.

Your initial meeting with your lawyer should tell you a great deal about him. First impressions are very important; this may be your only chance to impress your lawyer. Wear your best, dress neatly and comb your hair when you go to see him. State your case briefly; his time is valuable.

As likely as not, your lawyer will fall into one of the following categories:

TYPES OF LAWYERS

THE WARRIOR is ready to do battle even if there is nothing to fight about. Terms like "tactical error," "diversionary defense in depth" and "take to the field" come easy to him. The word "settlement" has yet to enter his vocabulary. His favorite expression: "In war, there is no substitute for victory."

THE HUMANITARIAN believes there's a place for human kindness even in legal practice. He is concerned about your state of mind; of all lawyers, this is the type most likely to tell you more than a day in advance that you are to appear in court. He commiserates with you about having lost the case but tells you not to worry. Your life is still ahead of you. His favorite expression: "Winning isn't everything."

THE SCHOLAR refers to even the smallest dispute as a "controversy arising under the law of the United States." His citings include quotes from opinions published by the Supreme Court, *The Federal Reporter, The Supplement* and *The National Reporter System.*

THE IDEALIST always wanted to be a lawyer and is not in it for the money, provided his bills get paid on time. He enjoys discussions about the ethics of the profession on your time. His favorite expression: "Truth will win out."

THE OPTIMIST is confident that everything will turn out all right even though the lower court ruled against you. He never gives up as long as you're still solvent. He is in favor of taking your case all the way to the Supreme Court. His favorite expression: "Tomorrow is another day."

THE PHILOSOPHER is always deep in thought. He makes it his policy never to voice an opinion, or riskier still, make a prediction as to the outcome of a case. In the months that follow he will caution you repeatedly against jumping to premature conclusions. His favorite expression: "Let's sleep on it."

THE HARD WORKER complains the loudest about the demands of the profession, his lack of time for his wife, his children and his mistress. He tells you no amount of money can make up for the loss of simple pleasures in his life. His favorite expression: "There are only twenty-four hours in a day."

THE COMEDIAN finds humor everywhere, including in his monthly fees, in the amount the court has just ordered you to pay and, especially, in you going into personal bankruptcy. His favorite expression: "You only live once. You may as well enjoy it."

THE INFLUENTIAL has three telephones on his desk, all within easy reach. He is able to use them all at the same time. He claims his success is due to his close attention to human relationships. His favorite expression: "It's not what you know..."

THE AUTHORITY rarely asks questions, and if he does, it's only to find out if you know the answer. Because he is intellectually superior to the people he deals with such as judges, colleagues and most of all, his clients, he is reluctant to go into depth on any subject, except that of his fees. His favorite expression: "You know your job, I know mine."

SUMMARY

1. Beware of the lawyer who tells jokes. The next joke may be on you.

2. Never trust a lawyer who sits up straight, looks you in the eye, tells you honesty is the best policy and wants to know how much money you make.

3. No lawyer ever goes to court unprepared. He is fully prepared to get paid for every minute he spends there.

4. Never talk about your lawyer at a dinner table and cause others to lose their appetites.

5. Being sued is no cause for alarm. Getting a lawyer to handle your case is.

Client's-at-a-Glance Guide

Here is a brief summary of the types of lawyers available to serve your legal needs. Their personalities may be as important as their disciplines. Also indicated for easy reference are their customary hourly rates.

	Type	Cost
	THE WARRIOR Contested divorce, personal injury, false arrest, debt collection, foreclosures.	Excessive.
	THE HUMANITARIAN Immigration, landlord/tenant litigation, worker's compensation, disability pension, child custody.	Excessive.
	THE SCHOLAR Constitutional law, corporate mergers, fraud, civil rights, international law, television talk shows.	Excessive.
	THE IDEALIST Environmental issues, consumer protection, animal rights, equal employment opportunity, police brutality.	Excessive.

	THE OPTIMIST Personal bankruptcy, labor disputes, premarital contracts, parole supervision, small business loans.	Excessive.
	THE PHILOSOPHER Judicial appeals, probate proceedings, tax audits, labor relations, political disputes, libel and slander defamation.	Excessive.
	THE COMEDIAN Uncontested divorce, plagiarism, defamation, obscenity, alienation of affections.	Excessive.
	THE HARD WORKER Marital disputes, suspension of a sentence, anti-trust, liability cases, estate planning, title search, Medicare/Medicaid matters, medical malpractice.	Excessive.
	THE INFLUENTIAL Labor disputes, loans, corporate mergers, international law.	Excessive.
	THE AUTHORITY Disposition of property, testamentary disposition.	Excessive.

About the Author

Among Stephen Baker's twenty-one books are over a dozen humor titles—including the best-sellers *How to Live with a Neurotic Cat*, *How to Live with a Neurotic Dog*, *How to Play Golf in the Low 120's*, *I Hate Meetings* and *How to Look Like Somebody in Business without Being Anybody*. In addition to his celebrated acclaim as an author, Baker is a renowned art director and adman, was twice nominated "Art Director of the Year," and has been the recipient of just about every award granted in print and television advertising. He is a columnist for *Advertising Age* and a much sought-after lecturer on creativity, advertising and publishing. He is perhaps most widely-known for his creation of one of America's best-recognized slogans, "Let Your Fingers Do the Walking," developed for an AT&T campaign. Baker currently lives in Manhattan, where he is at work on his next book. He maintains an office both in New York and Washington D.C. Some of his best friends—he insists—are lawyers.